MONUMENTAL MILESTONES
GREAT EVENTS OF MODERN TIMES

FDR and
the New Deal

A president of the people, Franklin Delano Roosevelt governed his fellow Americans from common ground.

Mitchell Lane
PUBLISHERS
P.O. Box 196
Hockessin, Delaware 19707

Titles in the Series

MONUMENTAL MILESTONES
GREAT EVENTS OF MODERN TIMES

FDR and
the New Deal

FDR's Emergency Railroad Transportation Act of 1933 attempted to revitalize a sagging railway industry and keep laborers "working on the railroad."

Earle Rice Jr.

PUBLISHERS

Printing   1   2   3   4   5   6   7   8   9

Library of Congress Cataloging-in-Publication Data
Rice, Earle.
  FDR and the New Deal / by Earle Rice, Jr.
      p. cm. — (Monumental milestones)
  Includes bibliographical references and index.
  ISBN 978-1-58415-828-8 (library bound)
  1. New Deal, 1933–1939—Juvenile literature. 2. United States—Politics and government—1933–1945—Juvenile literature. 3. Roosevelt, Franklin D. (Franklin Delano), 1882–1945—Juvenile literature. I. Title. II. Title: Franklin Delano Roosevelt and the New Deal.
  E806.R48 2010
  973.917—dc22
                                                                          2009027327

ABOUT THE AUTHOR: Earle Rice Jr. is a former senior design engineer and technical writer in the aerospace, electronic-defense, and nuclear industries. He has devoted full time to his writing since 1993 and is the author of more than sixty published books. Earle is listed in *Who's Who in America* and is a member of the Society of Children's Book Writers and Illustrators, the League of World War I Aviation Historians, the Air Force Association, and the Disabled American Veterans.

PUBLISHER'S NOTE: This story is based on the author's extensive research, which he believes to be accurate. Documentation of such research is contained on page 46.

The internet sites referenced herein were active as of the publication date. Due to the fleeting nature of some web sites, we cannot guarantee they will all be active when you are reading this book.

PLB

Contents

FDR and the New Deal

Earle Rice Jr.

*For Your Information

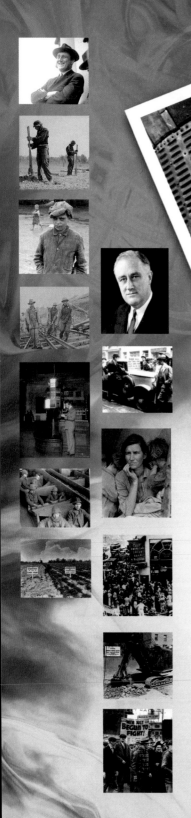

Dorothea Lange's 1936 photograph *Migrant Mother*

The photograph captured the look of anguish shared by thousands of American mothers caught up in the uncertainties of the Great Depression. It would be up to Franklin Delano Roosevelt to pull the country out of despair.

Good Times to Bad Times

In late October of 1929, the fortunes of three million Americans fell like so many autumn leaves on a windswept day. Few saw the financial calamity coming, though many should have. Symptoms of a flawed economic system had started to accumulate in the United States shortly after the end of World War I. During the Roaring Twenties, a decade of prosperity and excesses, warning signs went unnoticed—or at least unheeded.

Before World War I, American consumers had purchased most goods with cash. Beginning about 1923, however, enterprising lenders and providers introduced the concept of "buy now, pay later." Advertising agencies and merchants began to hype products of every description. Millions of eager Americans lined up to seize their share of "the good life" today rather than tomorrow.

By 1927, American consumers were purchasing about three-quarters of their furniture, phonographs, washing machines, and cars on credit. Installment buying accounted for more than half of all purchases of radios, pianos, sewing machines, vacuum cleaners, and refrigerators. In barely four years, borrowing against future earnings had become rooted in the American way of life.

Mortgaging their future paychecks for instant gratification worked well for many Americans, so long as the economy prospered. From 1921 to 1928, under U.S. presidents Warren G. Harding and Calvin Coolidge, a generally prosperous economy produced a rise in production. Increased production created more jobs. More workers produced more money for more purchases. Consumers—now used to credit spending—bought still more on payment plans. The economy spiraled upward on promises to pay. No one seemed to care that a reversal of this trend would send the economic spiral spinning downward.

As a leading indicator of America's prosperity in the 1920s, stock trading soared. Most analysts agree that the rise in stock prices was justified until early 1928. By then, however, the market had become a bubble. The prices paid by

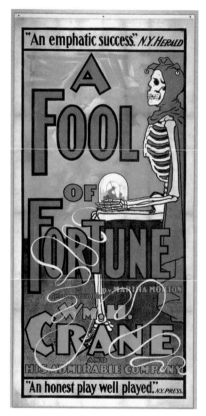

"An emphatic success." *N.Y. HERALD*

A **FOOL** OF **FORTUNE**

BY M. H. CRANE AND HIS ADMIRABLE COMPANY

"An honest play well played." *N.Y. PRESS.*

A poster for an 1890 stage play foretells the dangers of investing in the stock market.

investors had surpassed any reasonable expectation of future earnings. The first stirrings of trouble ahead were felt on the stock exchange in September 1929. Stock prices collapsed unexpectedly but recovered quickly.

Then, on Wednesday, October 23, a torrent of stock liquidations flooded the New York Stock Exchange. More than six million shares changed hands in the great hall at Broad and Wall Streets. The ticker that flashes transactions across the country fell two hours behind. Paper values of some four billion dollars were swept away before the close of trading. On Thursday morning, investors still held hopes for some miraculous reversal of fortune. It did not come.

"The market opened steady with prices little changed from the previous day, though some rather large blocks, of 20,000 to 25,000 shares, came out at the start," reported financial writer Elliott V. Bell. "It sagged easily for the first half-hour, and then around eleven o'clock the deluge broke."[1] Shares changed hands, continued Bell,

with a speed and ferocity that left men dazed. The bottom simply fell out of the market. From all over the country a torrent of selling orders poured onto the floor of the Stock Exchange and there were no buying orders to meet it. . . . Within a few moments the ticker service was hopelessly swamped and from then on no one knew what was really happening. . . . The last quotation was not printed on the tape until 7.08 1/2 P.M., four hours, eight and one-half minutes after the close. In the meantime, Wall Street had lived through an incredible nightmare.[2]

The stock market had fallen into absolute disarray. A record 12.9 million shares had traded hands. Several of New York's leading bankers tried to calm rapidly mounting fears with huge infusions of their own money. Newspapers around the nation joined in with assurances from the high and the mighty. President Herbert Hoover himself issued a White House statement to inspire confidence in the system. He reminded Americans: "The fundamental business of the country, that is, production and distribution of commodities, is on a sound and prosperous basis."[3] It was a fair evaluation based on what he knew at the time, but the financial situation remained in a state of flux.

Trading stabilized somewhat on Friday and Saturday, but prices began slipping again by session's end on Saturday. On Monday, panic set in again. Prices plunged. Steel dropped 17.5 points, General Electric 47.5, Allied Chemical 36, Westinghouse 34.5, and on it went. By day's end, it had become obvious that efforts by the bankers to halt the run on stocks had failed. But the worst would come the next day.

Pandemonium came crashing down on the Great Hall of the New York Stock Exchange on Tuesday, October 29, 1929. Toppling fortunes turned this empty chamber into a riotous throng of frenzied traders, as almost 13 million shares changed hands.

A lone Wall Street broker at his station in the vacant hall of the Stock Exchange

"Within half an hour of the opening the volume of trading had passed three million shares," wrote social historian Frederick Lewis Allen, "by twelve o'clock it had passed eight million, by half-past one it had passed twelve million, and when the closing gong brought the day's madness to an end the gigantic record of 16,410,030 shares had been set."[4] It was Tuesday, October 29, 1929—known then and ever afterward as Black Tuesday. It was the day that the stock market crashed and shook the world.

$$$

After the "crash of 1929," as the Wall Street meltdown came to be called, Americans entered into a decade of despair known as the Great Depression. One of the enduring myths of the twentieth century holds that the crash of the stock market caused the Depression. Most scholars agree, however, that it was only a symptom of long-term problems in the nation's economic system. The crash had burst the bubble of soaring stock prices, risky business ventures, and increased credit spending. It revealed—but did not create—the flaws in the economic system.

Historian Samuel Eliot Morison later observed, "Economic analysis, a science then in its infancy, failed to discern the serious faults in American and European economics and their increasing vulnerability to shock."[5] The true causes of the Depression were several and varied, and had been forming over the previous decade. Major causes included out-of-control speculation, reckless business expansion, and little oversight and loose regulation of the U.S. banking system. The surge in consumer credit spending added another stress factor. (Today, these contributors to economic collapse might seem all too familiar to many Americans.)

Moreover, the prosperity of the 1920s had not reached out to large sections of the nation. By decade's end, more than half of all American families lived on the edge of poverty. These struggling families were too poor to join the credit revolution. Eventually, manufacturers produced more goods than qualified consumers could purchase. An excess of goods caused an imbalance between supply and demand. This added to the strain on an already overburdened economy.

Because the crash occurred on President Herbert Hoover's watch (1929–1933), history has assigned much of the blame to him for the ensuing hard times. Hoover was a former mining engineer and U.S. secretary of commerce. At first, he thought that the economic downturn was one of a cyclical pattern. Recessions

Americans left with money after the Crash could find great bargains at the expense of those less fortunate.

More than three million Americans lost their fortunes in 1929. Overnight, investors in the stock market went from rich to poor. The Great Crash forced countless once-affluent men to sell almost all of their belongings just to provide food and shelter for their families.

had occurred periodically in America's past. He adopted a policy embodied in a comment once made by Democrat Grover Cleveland. With regard to the recession of 1893, Cleveland had said: "It is the business of the people to support the government, but it is not the business of the government to support the people."[6] Hoover's initial "do nothing" approach did not work, and he turned to a policy of partial intervention.

Shortly after the crash, Hoover called on business leaders not to lay off workers or to cut wages, and even to increase wages. He felt that maintaining wages was essential to restoring and sustaining prosperity. Hoover federalized parts of the credit system. He further tried to raise spending levels through government-sponsored action by business leaders. In 1930, he raised tariffs under the Smoot-Hawley Tariff Act—which actually worked against recovery efforts. Two years later, he signed into law the Revenue Act of 1932. It was then the largest peacetime tax hike in U.S. history.

In the summer of 1932, Hoover ordered the dispersal of the "Bonus Army" in Washington, D.C. Almost 20,000 World War I veterans and their families had

Construction began on the dam under Hoover in 1931 and ended under FDR in 1936. It was designated a National Historic Monument in 1985.

Hoover Dam, located 30 miles southeast of Las Vegas, Nevada, is a lasting tribute to its namesake, President Herbert Hoover.

camped near the Capitol to demand early payment of their bonuses. Army troops led by General Douglas MacArthur drove out the protesters and burned their camp. An enraged public outcry erased whatever chances remained for Hoover's reelection later that year.

On the plus side, Hoover initiated public works construction on the San Francisco Bay Bridge, the Los Angeles Aqueduct, and the Hoover Dam. He finally supported relief to farmers through the Reconstruction Finance Corporation. The Federal Home Loan Bank Act, passed in 1932, ranked high among his achievements. It helped hard-pressed homeowners to avoid foreclosure.

President Hoover's best efforts failed to lead the nation out of economic decline, and the nation plunged deeper into depression. His critics say—arguably—that the solutions he offered failed because he did not use the full resources of the government. In any event, millions of Americans began to call for a new approach to the worsening situation. New York Governor Franklin Delano Roosevelt answered their call for new solutions.

By the spring and summer of 1932, President Herbert Hoover had become convinced of the need to balance the federal budget. Unless the government paid its own bills, he felt, a general loss of confidence would undermine all his measures against the Depression. A balanced budget, Hoover declared, was "the most essential factor to recovery"; further, it was "the foundation of all public and private financial stability."[7]

Hoover's new emphasis on fiscal responsibility came at a time when the federal deficit stood at more than two billion dollars. Moreover, anti-Depression spending had increased while tax revenue was declining. Clearly, it would require drastic action of some sort to replace federal red ink with black. The Revenue Act of 1932 represented one attempt to set the federal balance sheets in order. It proved to be wholly counterproductive.

President Hoover

Two weeks later, Congress voted to refuse early payment of $2.4 billion in bonuses to World War I veterans. (The bonuses had been approved by Congress in 1924 for disbursement in 1945.) In June 1932, an army of some 20,000 veterans and their families marched on Washington in protest. They called themselves the Bonus Expeditionary Force. Hoover ordered the U.S. Army to evict the "Bonus Marchers" (or "Bonus Army") from several federal buildings they had occupied on Pennsylvania Avenue. General Douglas MacArthur led the operation, assisted by Dwight D. Eisenhower and George S. Patton.

MacArthur accomplished his mission with unfortunate results: two marchers were shot dead. Acting on his own authority, he continued on to the shantytown set up by the marchers in nearby Anacostia. He dispersed the marchers and their families using tear gas, then put the torch to their encampment. An eleven-week-old baby died from the gas. Hoover's hopes for reelection in the fall died with her.

The burning of the
Bonus Marchers' shantytown

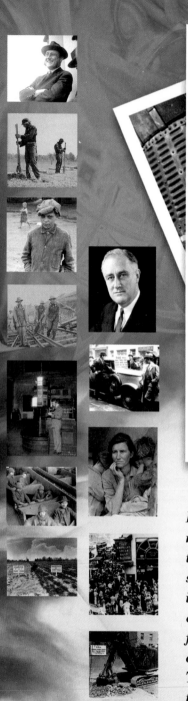

Depositors gather outside New York Union Bank during a bank run earl Depression.

Fear of bank failures sent millions of Americans swarming to banks to withdraw their savings. Bankers began calling in loans and selling assets to counter the sudden loss of funds. A depressed market drove down the value of assets. The resulting liquidity crisis threatened to crush the U.S. banking system and economy.

CHAPTER 2

FDR

At ten o'clock on the night of July 1, 1932, Democrats nominated Franklin Delano Roosevelt as their candidate for president of the United States. The next day, FDR—as he was popularly known—flew in to Chicago on a silvery Ford Tri-Motor airplane to address their convention. Historically, the party's nominee did not accept its nomination at the convention. Later that evening, FDR became the first presidential nominee to break with tradition. His breach of a longstanding practice stands as only one unconventional action among many he would undertake in the days to come.

In his acceptance speech at Chicago Stadium, Roosevelt said, "Let it from now on be the task of our Party to break foolish traditions. . . . I pledge you, I pledge myself, to a new deal for the American people. . . . This is more than a political campaign; it is a call to arms."[1] "The very next day," observed FDR scholar William E. Leuchtenburg, "an alert cartoonist plucked from Roosevelt's speech the words 'new deal'—a phrase to which the Governor had attached no special significance—and henceforth they were to be the hallmark of the Roosevelt program."[2]

In the fall of 1932, Americans rallied behind FDR's "call to arms" and swept him into the highest office in the land. In a landslide victory over Herbert Hoover, Roosevelt received 22.8 million popular votes and 472 electoral votes to Hoover's respective votes of 15.7 million and 59. The United States stood on the threshold of a new president, a new era, and a New Deal.

Franklin Delano Roosevelt, the nation's thirty-second president, took office facing enormous problems. Between his election in November 1932 and his inauguration in March 1933, the American banking system had shut down completely. In addition to the deepening worldwide Depression, the winds of war had begun to blow in Europe and Asia. Japan had seized Manchuria from China in 1931. The following year, it established the puppet state of Manchukuo in East Asia. Amid the despair brought on by massive unemployment, the Germans installed future dictator Adolf Hitler as chancellor early in 1933. Future militant aspirations of Japan and Germany would bear watching, but hard times at home demanded FDR's immediate attention.

The people had overwhelmingly chosen FDR to lead them out of hard times—a man who had never in his life wanted for a single thing. Hoover had worked his way through Stanford University to become a mining engineer and self-made millionaire. Roosevelt was born into a family that had enjoyed wealth for several generations. He never lacked the doting affection of family. His father, James Roosevelt, maintained the family inheritance through ventures in railroads and coal mining. James never let business interfere with his enjoyment of the family estate at Hyde Park on New York's Hudson River. He likewise enjoyed sailing in the waters around the Canadian island of Campobello, where he built a summer home.

In 1880, four years after the death of his first wife, James met and married Sara Delano. At the age of twenty-six, the strikingly beautiful Sara was exactly half his age. She was the daughter of another well-to-do family of the local gentry and the fifth cousin of Theodore Roosevelt, the twenty-sixth president of the United States. On January 30, 1882, Sara bore James a son, Franklin. During their son's early years, James would pass along to him his love of country living and the importance of noblesse oblige—the idea that privilege entails responsibility to those less fortunate. From his mother, Franklin would acquire an unshakable self-confidence and calm—and probably a streak of aloofness and arrogance that sometimes offended others.

Young Franklin Roosevelt grew up in the Hudson Valley as a privileged member of a wealthy family.

Franklin grew up in the Hudson Valley amid an abundance of material things. Private tutors provided his early education. In 1896, at age fourteen, he continued his education away from home at the exclusive Groton School in Massachusetts. The Reverend Endicott Peabody, the school's founder and headmaster, infused a classical curriculum with moral significance. He instilled in Franklin and his classmates a high sense of the importance of Christian responsibility.

In the fall of 1900, Franklin entered Harvard University. On December 8, his father died at age seventy-two. Sara noted his passing in her diary the next day: "All is over. At 2:20 he merely slept away."[3] Franklin returned to Harvard after New Year's, where he lived an active athletic and social life. Though never an outstanding scholar, he prided himself on serving as editor of the *Crimson*, the undergraduate newspaper. While at Harvard, he became interested in politics and joined the Harvard Republican Club. He cast his first vote for his cousin Theodore Roosevelt in the presidential election of 1904. After graduating from Harvard in just three years, Franklin entered Columbia Law School in New York City.

Sometime during his Harvard years, Franklin had begun courting Eleanor Roosevelt, a distant cousin. She was the daughter of Elliott and Anna Hall Roosevelt and the niece of Theodore Roosevelt. Eleanor was known as the "ugly duckling" of the family. She once said of herself, "I knew I was the first girl in my mother's family who was not a belle."[4] Their mutual attraction appeared more intellectual than physical. Nevertheless, their romance—which seemed odd to many—blossomed, and they were married on March 17, 1905. Cousin "Teddy" flew to New York from Washington, D.C., to give away the bride. After the ceremony, he said, "Well, Franklin, there's nothing like keeping the name in the family."[5]

In 1907, Franklin passed the New York bar examinations. He did not bother to finish his degree at Columbia, a not-uncommon practice at the time. After practicing law for the next three years, he decided to enter politics. In 1910, Franklin won election to the New York State Senate as a Democrat in a heavily Republican district. His impressive victory caught the eye of Woodrow Wilson, the newly elected governor of New Jersey.

Two years later, Wilson won the presidential election of 1912. He called on Franklin to serve as assistant secretary of the navy. His cousin Teddy had held the post under President William McKinley. Franklin accepted and served with dedication and efficiency as assistant secretary throughout World War I. He reported to Secretary of the Navy Josephus Daniels, who had recommended him for the post. Daniels admired Franklin and noted in his diary: "His distinguished cousin TR went from the place to the presidency. May history repeat itself."[6]

At the start of the 1920s, Franklin's political future looked bright. His party named him as vice-presidential candidate on the Democratic ticket with Governor James M. Cox of Ohio. Republican Warren G. Harding won the election, but Franklin remained active in politics. Then, suddenly, polio struck him down. Polio, short for poliomyelitis (poh-lee-oh-my-uh-LYT-iss), then commonly known as infantile paralysis, is an infectious viral disease that often produces temporary or permanent paralysis.

Lesser men might have surrendered to the crippling disease, but Franklin persevered. He fought through the pain and rigors of physical therapy. Though never again able to walk unassisted, he resumed his political career with the aid of braces and a wheelchair. In a time before twenty-four-hour television news coverage, he kept his infirmity out of the public eye for the most part. Photographs and newsreels in which he appeared usually concealed his braces and wheelchair and depicted him looking vigorous and robust.

At the Democratic National Convention in 1928, Franklin nominated New York governor Alfred E. Smith for president. Franklin himself ran for Smith's soon-to-be-vacant governor's seat. Smith lost to Herbert Hoover in a landslide, but Franklin won by a slim margin. His political capital soared. Governor Harry F. Byrd of Virginia told him, "You are the hope of the Democratic party."[7] The crash of '29 tumbled down during Franklin's first year in office, soon followed by the Great Depression. The Democrats—and more importantly, the American people and the nation—would need every scrap of hope available.

While serving the needs of New York State, Franklin used his years as governor to experiment with the kinds of programs that would later prove useful at a national level. At the same time, he put together a team of effective leaders who would join him in serving the nation in Washington, D.C. The list of notables included Henry Morgenthau Jr., Frances Perkins, Harry Hopkins, and others.

In 1932, when first the Democrats and then the American people called on him to lead the nation out of the doldrums of depression, Franklin Delano Roosevelt was ready. Undaunted by the desperate times and frightened masses, FDR told the nation with calm assurance at his inauguration, "The only thing we have to fear is fear itself."[8]

Franklin D. Roosevelt cut a dashing figure as a young man, handsome, charming, and filled with a zest for living. Eleanor Roosevelt, his distant cousin and future soul mate, grew up thinking of herself as an ugly duckling. She perhaps should have thought more kindly of herself. Roosevelt scholar Arthur M. Schlesinger Jr. wrote that Franklin "admired her intelligence, integrity, and sympathy; and doubtless he was captivated by her lustrous eyes, her vivid smile, and her willowy grace."[9] The sadness of her childhood had much to do with her sorrowful self-appraisal.

Elliott Roosevelt, Eleanor's father, suffered from severe bouts of alcoholism. Anna Hall Roosevelt, her stunningly beautiful mother, never accepted her for being female and physically unattractive. She once told Eleanor, "You're so plain that you really have nothing to do except be good."[10] Before Eleanor turned ten years old, her mother, father, and one of her two brothers had died.

With the death of her parents, Eleanor's care reverted to her grandmother, and her education to a governess. They provided little more than stern discipline and additional criticism. At age fifteen, Eleanor was sent abroad to a French school near London run by a remarkable woman named Marie Souvestre. There she finally found some happiness and recaptured her self-confidence.

Soon after Eleanor returned to New York in 1902, she began dating her distant cousin Franklin, and they fell in love. They wed three years later. She eventually bore her husband six children (one of whom died in infancy). Their marriage appeared loving and stable. Then, during World War I, Eleanor discovered Franklin's affair with her personal secretary, Lucy Mercer. Eleanor offered to divorce him but agreed to remain married, as a divorce would have ruined Franklin's political career. Thereafter their marriage was devoid of romance, but they went on to form a unique and powerful political alliance.

Eleanor Roosevelt became an influential figure in her own right. She supported liberal causes, wrote a newspaper column ("My Day") and several books, and served as a U.S. delegate to the United Nations General Assembly.

Eleanor Roosevelt
at the United Nations

FDR endeared himself to the American a series of friendly radio broadcast known as "fireside chats."

On March 12, 1933, *utilizing the still-new medium of radio, FDR initiated a series of talks on public policy issues. Addressing his radio audience as "my friends," his relaxed delivery of plainly worded text won the support of millions of Americans for many of his New Deal policies. FDR continued his friendly, informative "fireside chats" throughout his presidency (1933–1945).*

The New Deal:
The First Hundred Days

Franklin Delano Roosevelt delivered his inaugural address as the thirty-second president of the United States to a rain-soaked audience on March 4, 1933. The gloom of the day matched the mood of a nation mired in economic depression. But the oratorical splendor of the new president's words brightened the faces of his onlookers like sunlight after rain. His speech inspired a nation with new hope and confidence.

In ringing tones, FDR told the crowd before the Capitol that he would call a special session of Congress to consider ways to end America's economic crisis. Should Congress have no answers, he said, he was prepared to boldly lead the nation in a new direction: "I shall ask the Congress for the one remaining instrument to meet the crisis—broad Executive power to wage a war against the emergency, as great as the power that would be given to me if we were in fact invaded by a foreign foe."[1] The crowd responded with thunderous applause. And FDR began his first hundred days in office.

FDR had no plan as such to remedy the nation's ills. Malcolm Cowley, author and literary editor of *The New Republic*, called him a "happy experimentalist."[2] FDR recognized the need for quick action, and he acted quickly and boldly. His natural charm and ability in the new arena of public relations enabled him to put in place and implement a variety of stopgap measures to stem the public bleeding and build public confidence. Right off, he held an unparalleled number of press conferences, hired the first presidential press secretary, and initiated a series of radio broadcasts he liked to call "fireside chats." By keeping citizens informed, FDR eased their suffering and restored their faith in Washington. Most important, he made Americans feel that they were an integral part of the recovery process.

On his first day in office, FDR declared a national "bank holiday" and proposed the Emergency Banking Act. Congress passed the measure on March 9. Without nationalizing the banks, the act provided federal assistance to reopen banks with certified solvency. After examination, uncertified banks were placed in the hands of federal "conservators" to help them regain solvency. The act helped restore public confidence in the U.S. banking system. It also granted sweeping fiscal powers to FDR.

The Emergency Banking Act officially took the United States off the gold standard. It made owning gold illegal, except in jewelry and the like. Also, it raised the value of the dollar abroad and made it no longer redeemable in gold. As the first enacted legislation of FDR's New Deal, it represented an early indication of the mammoth role that government was about to play in the private affairs of Americans.

In the economic crisis of 2008–2009, U.S. Presidents George W. Bush and Barack H. Obama presided over similar legislation to "bail out" U.S. banks in trouble and "stimulate" the economy. Under President Bush, Congress authorized $700 billion in bank aid as part of the Troubled Assets Recovery Plan in October 2008. Four months later, Congress passed the American Recovery and Reinvestment Act. Better known as President Obama's stimulus plan (or package), it provided $787 billion to "jump-start" the American economy. The huge sums sent to rescue banks and boost the economy—calculated to grow much larger when interest was added—exceed any other such costs in American history. They are largely borne by the American taxpayer. The effectiveness of such high-risk solutions to today's complex financial and economic crises will probably not be known for years to come.

FDR aired his first fireside chat on March 12. He informed the American public of government efforts to get the U.S. banking system back on track. Further, he assured depositors that any bank opening the next day would be solvent and approved by the government. By week's end, customers had returned more than $600 million in hoarded currency to the banks; by the end of March, nearly $1 billion. Educator and political adviser Raymond Moley noted later that American capitalism "was saved in eight days."[3]

Additional New Deal legislation gushed out of Congress like water from a fractured dam. "Roosevelt's New Deal programs were most remarkable for their number and their commitment to making government an active instrument in ensuring social justice," wrote historian Douglas G. Brinkley. "The new president asked Congress to pass the Economy Act, which reduced federal salaries by as much as 15 percent and together with other cost-cutting measures carved some $243 million from the federal budget."[4] The act became law on March 20. Two days later, Congress, anticipating the repeal of Prohibition (which outlawed alcoholic beverages), enacted the Beer-Wine Revenue Act to enhance federal coffers.

During FDR's last year as governor of New York, he had conceived the idea of sending jobless men to work in forests. As president, he envisioned a conservation army of a million young men working for a dollar a day. In mid-March, FDR outlined his plan to Raymond Moley and said, "I think I'll go ahead with this—the way I did with beer"[5] (referring to the Beer-Wine Revenue Act).

Congress passed the Civilian Conservation Corps Reforestation Act, establishing the Civilian Conservation Corps. It provided some 250,000 jobs for young men between the ages of 18 and 25. They earned thirty dollars a month (part of which went to dependents). More than two million young men would serve by 1941. They accounted for more than half of all forest planting—public and private—in the nation's history.

Moving ahead swiftly, Congress established the Federal Emergency Relief Agency on May 12 and authorized $500 million to be granted (not loaned) to state and local agencies. FDR appointed Harry Hopkins to head FERA, as it was called. Hopkins had managed a similar state agency under FDR in New York. Later, as head of the Civil Works Administration, Hopkins found ways to utilize 4.2 million unemployed workers on a budget of only $400 million. He paid them with minimum wages for useful work rather than with relief checks for doing nothing. The workers built schools, playgrounds, athletic fields, roads, public buildings, airports, and more.

Also on May 12, Congress passed the Agricultural Adjustment Act. It boosted farm prices by limiting crop cultivation and livestock breeding. Directed by Henry Wallace, the secretary of agriculture, it also enabled currency inflation through silver coinage, paper, and other forms of currency. Six days later, on May 18, Washington lawmakers created the Tennessee Valley Authority. Congress charged this federal agency with controlling floods, improving navigation, and generating electric power along the Tennessee River. Passage of the Securities Act on May 27 completed legislative activity for the month. This act required corporations and investment bankers to file statements of full disclosure with the Federal Trade Commission for stocks offered for sale.

The flurry of new legislation swept on into June. Lawmakers enacted the Home Owners' Loan Act on June 13. Through the Home Owners' Loan Corporation, the government entered into the business of refinancing home loans. It thereby rescued homeowners from foreclosure and prevented the further collapse of mortgage lending institutions. By the mid-1930s, the Home Owners' Loan Corpora-

A dust storm threatens to explode across a small Midwestern town.

From 1932 to 1940, in the region of the Great Plains known as the Dust Bowl, severe drought and poor agricultural practices contributed to ferocious dust storms that suffocated people and cattle and destroyed crops.

In addition to building dams and power plants, the Tennessee Valley Authority produced chemical fertilizers for farmers. Under the TVA, the replenishment of soil and improved farming techniques restored worn-out fields to productive farmlands.

A TVA photograph illustrates the sharp contrast between unfertilized lands and lands fertilized with phosphate and lime.

tion would refinance nearly 20 percent of the nation's homes. Three days later, Congress extended similar assistance to farm owners via the Farm Credit Act, which created the Farm Credit Administration. Managed by Henry Morgenthau Jr., it refinanced more than one-fifth of the country's farms within the next eighteen months.

That same day, June 16, Congress passed the Banking Act (Glass-Steagall Act) to further regulate banks. This act widened the Federal Reserve Board's power over banks. It also prohibited commercial banks from engaging in investment banking. Through the Federal Deposit Insurance Corporation, the Banking Act guaranteed deposits to a fixed amount (now permanently $100,000 but temporarily raised to $250,000 through December 31, 2009) in member banks of the Federal Reserve System.

Last, also on June 16, FDR signed the National Industrial Recovery Act into law. It created the National Recovery Administration, which established fair trade codes—government-supervised self-regulation by industries. New regulations

"Breaker boys" separate slate rock from coal in a Pennsylvania coal mine.

Sons of miners between the ages of 8 and 13, these breaker boys often worked 14 to 16 hours a day. They became the focus of activists campaigning for child labor laws.

called for restrictions on plant operations, minimum wages of twelve to thirteen dollars a week, no child labor, a forty-hour work week, and other worker-friendly requirements. *The United Mine Workers Journal* called the National Recovery Administration "the greatest victory for labor that ever was achieved."[6] Much later, the U.S. Supreme Court ruled some elements of the act unconstitutional. The Recovery Act also created the Public Works Administration, with a $3.3 million budget for building highways, federal buildings, and military installations.

Congress recessed later that day—June 16, 1933—and FDR's first hundred days in office ended. Political columnist Walter Lippmann, who had earlier dismissed FDR as a political lightweight, now lauded the president. "At the end of February," he wrote, "we were a congeries [collection] of disorderly panic-stricken mobs and factions. In a hundred days from March to June we became an organized nation confident of our power to provide for our own security and to control our own destiny."[7]

The Great Depression of the 1930s was the worst depression in the history of the United States. It began with the collapse of the stock market in October 1929 and lingered for more than a decade. Overextended credit spending, inflated stock prices, and many other factors toppled the U.S. financial system like sand castles in a raging surf.

Economist John K. Galbraith once observed, "One of the uses of depression is to expose what the auditors fail to find."[8] The Depression revealed fissures in the U.S. economy and brought dramatic changes to the American way of life. It shook American confidence and led to a restructuring of the economy; new relations between government, business, and labor; and greater federal involvement in the economy and social welfare.

Young faces of the Great Depression wore expressions beyond their years.

American production went into decline in the summer of 1929 and continued to fall off after the stock market collapse in October. Less production caused the jobless rate to rise drastically, leaving an estimated 13 to 17 million workers unemployed by 1932 (or roughly one quarter of the labor force). Jobless young men (and a few women) took to the railways and highways in search of work. The homeless lived in shantytowns called "Hoovervilles" (named for then-President Herbert Hoover), that sprang up at the outskirts of towns.

Private and government charities quickly proved incapable of caring for the massive numbers of people seeking aid. Half of the unemployed came from eight states; a third came from highly industrialized Illinois, New York, Ohio, and Pennsylvania. Forty percent of those receiving relief were children. In the midst of the devastation, hamburgers sold two for a nickel. Workers making ten cents an hour could not afford them. Even with dirt-cheap labor, businesses could not make a profit. Interest rates plunged to less than 1 percent. Investors looked the other way, as few with money were willing to risk it in an unstable economy. Farmers let crops rot in the fields amidst a world plagued with hunger.

FDR and the New Deal tried to rescue the economy with great sums of money and huge government programs. But the Great Depression stubbornly dragged on for year after wearying year, until war finally brought back prosperity—but at a high price.

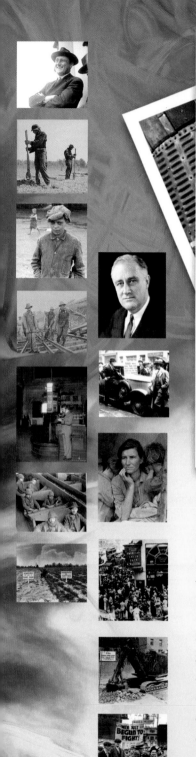

Digging post holes and stringing fences was all in a day's work in the life of a CCC member.

Congress created the Civilian Conservation Corps within a month of FDR's inauguration. Formed to provide work for men between the ages of 18 and 35, it was organized and run as a quasi-military body. CCC members worked at preventing and fighting forest fires, eradicating pests, building roads and bridges, setting in fences and firebreaks, and many other useful jobs.

CHAPTER 4

The New Deal:
The Second Time Around

Congress passed most of the major New Deal legislation in the first hundred days of FDR's administration. Much more legislation followed, however. It came at a less strenuous pace in the fall of 1933 and over the first six months of 1934. FDR established the Civil Works Administration under Harry Hopkins on November 9, 1933. The Civil Works Administration provided emergency unemployment relief. It created four million federal, state, and local "make-work" projects. During its five-month existence, it pumped about a billion dollars of purchasing power into the slumping economy.

Notable measures passed in 1934 included the Securities Exchange Act on June 6, the Communications Act on June 19, and the National Housing Act on June 28. The Securities Exchange Act created the Securities Exchange Commission to regulate the stock markets. Similarly, the Communications Act established the Federal Communications Commission to regulate the radio, telegraph, and cable businesses. Under the National Housing Act, the Federal Housing Administration insured home loans made by private lending institutions.

Through the leadership and programs of FDR and his "New Dealers," Americans found relief and new hope. The nation's gross national product (GNP) rose from $56 billion in 1933 to $72 billion in 1935. (GNP represents the total market value of the goods and services produced by a nation's economy during a specific period of time, such as a year.) Democrats capitalized on their New Deal successes. They swept the midterm congressional elections in 1934 and gained thirteen seats for FDR's party. But by then some twenty million people were receiving public assistance, and the welfare roles were increasing. "By the end of 1934," wrote William E. Leuchtenburg, "the government had spent over two billion dollars on relief, and Roosevelt felt he had little to show for it."[1]

In January 1935, the president told Congress that he wanted to replace relief programs with work opportunities. "I am not willing that the vitality of our people be further sapped by the giving of cash, of market baskets, of a few hours of weekly work cutting grass, raking leaves or picking up papers in public parks," FDR declared. "The Federal Government must and shall quit the business of relief."[2] Toward this end, he proposed the creation of a Works Progress Administration to replace earlier relief programs. His proposal ushered in a period of renewed legislation that political observers sometimes call the "Second New Deal."

On April 8, 1935, Congress passed the Emergency Relief Appropriation Act, authorizing the creation of the Works Progress Administration. FDR called Harry Hopkins over from the Federal Emergency Relief Agency to direct it. In its first two years, the Works Progress Administration oversaw the construction of 36,000 miles of rural roads, 5,800 mobile libraries, 3,300 dams, 1,654 medical and dental clinics, 1,634 school buildings, and 105 airport landing fields. Workers received roughly fifty dollars a month, about twice the amount they would have received on relief.

The Works Progress Administration would employ 8.5 million people and spend more than $11 billion in employment relief before being canceled in 1943. Though more expensive than direct relief programs, Hopkins believed the work relief program was worth it. "Give a man a dole," he explained, "and you save his body and destroy his spirit. Give him a job and you save both body and spirit."[3]

In 1938, the Works Progress Administration's peak year, women made up 13.5 percent

of its workers. Federal support also went out to tens of thousands of artists, sculptors, actors, writers, and musicians. "Hell! They've got to eat just like other people,"[4] quipped Hopkins. The program's support of the arts led to the creation of the National Foundation of the Arts and the National Endowment for the Arts.

With the passage of the Rural Electrification Act on May 11, 1935, Congress funded federal efforts to electrify hamlets and farmsteads. In the late summer, the Public Utility Holding Company Act, enacted on August 26, broke up the thirteen companies that then controlled most of the nation's utilities. Electricity prices dropped. Four days later, FDR's Revenue Act (better known as the "Wealth Tax") increased taxes on corpora-

tions and the rich. Together, these three laws siphoned corporate capital while boosting the incomes of the poorest Americans. (Informed observers may recognize some similarities between certain New Deal enactments and the provisions of

President Barack Obama's stimulus package of 2009. Critics of Obama's tax plan complained that it fostered a "redistribution of wealth.") Overall, the two most important laws to come out of the Second New Deal were the Social Security Act and the National Labor Relations Act.

The Social Security Act, enacted on August 14, enrolled more than half of all Americans in a federal pension program that guaranteed them a retirement income. It also provided funds to states for unemployment and disability insurance. Single mothers of dependent children also received aid from Social Security funding. "With the Social Security Act," observed historian Arthur M. Schlesinger

Striking United Auto Workers stood up and later sat down for their rights in Flint, Michigan, from 1936 to 1937.

The "sitdown strike" protested dismal working conditions. Singing "Solidarity Forever" and sharing simple meals of bean soup, apples, and bread, they banded together in sacrifice and won new rights for workers.

Jr., "the constitutional dedication of federal power to the general welfare began a new phase of national history."[5] The Social Security Act laid the base on which the American welfare state was built.

Few, if any, measures have had a greater impact on American labor than has the National Labor Relations Act (or "Wagner Act"). Enacted on July 5, 1935, it guaranteed the right of workers to organize and bargain collectively. It created the National Labor Relations Board to oversee collective bargaining and prevent unfair labor practices. Most important, it opened the door to unionism in mass-production industries. "Organized labor would play a key role in the New Deal's welfare state," notes historian Michael E. Parrish, "a larger role than labor had ever played before in the nation's public policies—but it remained nonetheless a subordinate role."[6] (The federal bailout of U.S. automakers in 2008 focused new attention on the power wielded by unions.)

Despite the sweeping changes made by the Second New Deal, it stopped short of what some supporters had hoped to achieve. (The failure to adopt a national healthcare plan represents a solid case in point.) But its legislation left little doubt as to the direction in which it was taking the nation: it defined the role of government in American life for the rest of the century. The State fashioned by FDR and his New Dealers regulated and revitalized the economy, championed workers' rights, and extended welfare to the poor. For decades thereafter, political debate would no longer center on whether government should take a hand in economic and social affairs, but rather on how and how much.

Some of the New Deal legislation violated the United States Constitution. On May 27, 1935, the Supreme Court delivered two landmark decisions. It ruled that both the National Recovery Administration and the president's authority to remove members of the Federal Trade Commission were unconstitutional. In January 1936, the Court invalidated the Agricultural Adjustment Administration. This agency, as well as the National Recovery Administration, had not worked out well. Thus the Court had essentially spared FDR the embarrassment of having to cancel them himself.

The following year, FDR asked Congress to increase the number of justices on the Supreme Court. That would allow him to appoint justices more attuned to his policies. Amid a storm of protest, Roosevelt's detractors accused him of trying to "pack the Court." Congress rejected his request in July 1937. Because of his efforts to upset the ideological balance of the Court, FDR's reputation suffered lasting political damage.

At home, after the New Deal's second round of legislation, Democrats emerged as the nation's majority party. FDR handily defeated Kansas governor Alfred M. Landon in the presidential

OH, SO THAT'S THE KIND OF A SAILOR HE IS!

From March 22, 1937

Stricken with poliomyelitis (a paralyzing viral disease) at age 39, FDR prevailed on the press to refrain from publishing photographs revealing his disability. As a result of his "gentlemen's understanding" with the press, only a few candid photos have survived.

A rare photograph of FDR, his dog Fala, and little Ruthie Bie, a daughter of one of the workers on the Roosevelt estate.

election of 1936. His party swept the "Solid South" and urban America. In so doing, the Democrats won over the African American vote from the Republicans, and they came away with a large majority in the House and Senate. Abroad, the New Dealers orchestrated a shift in foreign policy: they initiated the "Good Neighbor Policy"—basically ending U.S. interventionist policies in Latin America—and promoted reciprocal trade agreements.

In summarizing FDR's role in the New Deal, historian David M. Kennedy wrote: "He did mend the evils of the Depression by reasoned experiment within the framework of the existing social system. He did prevent a naked confrontation between orthodoxy [convention] and revolution. The priceless value of that achievement, surely as much as the columns of ciphers that recorded national income and production, must be reckoned in any final accounting of what the New Deal did."[7]

Millions of Americans came to know and revere Franklin Delano Roosevelt through his regular fireside chats. He addressed his radio audience as "my friends." His relaxed delivery and plain speaking won the esteem of untold listeners across the nation. Their affection and admiration empowered him. In return, he accomplished much on their behalf during the New Deal era. But his achievements did not happen in a vacuum. Many opponents of FDR's policies raised their voices in dissent.

Socialist Norman Thomas, for example, strongly criticized abuses against tenant farmers and sharecroppers under the Agricultural Adjustment Act. Many were driven from their lands and cheated of their fair share of benefits by landlords and corrupt officials. In criticizing the National Recovery Act, U.S. Communist Party leader Earl Browder called it "the same as Hitler's program."[8]

Senator Huey "Kingfish" Long

Father Charles E. Coughlin hosted a Sunday-night radio program. Known as the "radio priest," he used the airwaves to promote silver holdings and foment anti-Semitism. He called the National Recovery Act and the Agricultural Adjustment Act "abortive."[9] The gentler voice of Dr. Francis Townsend, a California physician, offered elders the security of his Old Age Revolving Pensions, Limited. Feeling pressure from supporters of the "Townsend Plan," Congress opted instead to go with the Social Security Act.

Louisiana political leader and presidential wannabe Huey Long perhaps spoke loudest among the New Deal's voices of dissent. Critical of the National Recovery Act, he denounced it as a sham. "Every fault of socialism is to be found in this bill, without one of its virtues," he railed. "Every crime of monarchy is in here, without one of the things that would give it credit."[10] Curiously, as a U.S. senator, he ultimately voted for it. Long, popularly known as the Kingfish, planned to run for president in 1935. Sadly for him, a political assassin's bullet ended his candidacy and his life in September of that year.

Heavy equipment breaks ground at construction site in Washington, D.C.

The National Recovery Act of 1933 created the Public Works Administration (PWA) as part of FDR's massive New Deal legislation. It was designed to put Americans back to work during the Great Depression. With a budget of $3.3 billion, the PWA funded some 34,000 construction projects and created millions of jobs from 1933 to 1939.

CHAPTER 5

The New American Way

The presidential election of 1936 marked FDR's last big triumph of the New Deal era. He defeated Kansas governor Alfred M. Landon by the lopsided electoral-college margin of 523–8. His easy victory reaffirmed journalist William Allen White's earlier observation. After the midterm elections of 1934, White had written: "He has been all but crowned by the people."[1] Further, unemployment was down, and the economy seemed to be on the mend. But FDR faced a new dip in the Great Depression in the fall of 1937.

FDR felt that voters had given him a mandate in November 1936 to balance the federal budget. At the start of his second term, he moved to cut government spending. He counted on adding additional revenue through new taxes. In 1936, government spending had totaled $8.4 billion. FDR's spending cuts reduced spending to $7.7 billion in 1937. A year later, spending dropped to $6.8 billion.

In 1938, the economy proved more fragile than FDR and his advisers had thought. It was still weak and reliant upon government funds for fiscal support. The president's cutbacks resulted in the sharpest economic contraction in U.S. history, and critics quickly derided the New Deal as a failure. Its detractors included moderate Democrats who still resented his attempt to "pack the Court" early in 1937. The New Deal coalition began to come apart.

British economist John Maynard Keynes called FDR's spending cuts "an error of optimism."[2] Keynes recommended renewed spending on public works to help reverse the downturn. He also pointed out that the United States needed the help of private enterprise to solve its problems. FDR met his suggestions halfway. In the spring of 1938, he asked Congress to resume funding public works programs. He conceded that funding "began to taper off too quickly"[3] in 1937. Congress obliged. FDR abandoned fiscal responsibility and resumed a deliberate policy of deficit spending. He pushed through a new $4.5 billion package. It financed additional public housing and highway construction. FDR used part of the funding to bolster relief agencies.

In the first half of 1938, FDR herded two more measures through Congress. The Agricultural Adjustment Act of 1938 passed on February 16. It allowed the government to pay farmers for not planting crops. After strong resistance, FDR finally won passage of the Fair Labor Standards Act on June 25. The bill established minimum wages and maximum hours. It also banned child labor. Its passage signaled the end of New Deal legislation. FDR then addressed the labor bill's two major opponents—organized business and conservative southern Democrats.

President Roosevelt blamed the sharp economic downturn primarily on the unwillingness of businesses to work with New Deal monetary policies. Influenced by labor and the left, he felt that business and financial interests had done little to help improve the economy. He told his advisers that he was "sick and tired of being told . . . by everybody . . . what's the matter with the country and nobody suggests what I should do."[4] Angered by the lack of cooperation from businesses, FDR named firebrand Thurman Arnold to head the antitrust division of the Justice Department. Over the next five years, Arnold brought 230 lawsuits against corporations charged with running monopolies.

At the same time, FDR called on Congress to establish the Temporary National Economic Committee. He wanted the group to evaluate the economy and recommend options for its reform and recovery. After three years of study, the group recommended that the government spend more to encourage consumer purchasing. But it came up with no clear proposals for dealing with monopolies that controlled American businesses.

Political adviser Raymond Moley noted sourly that FDR's request for a study commission had represented little more than a delaying tactic. He called it "the final expression of Roosevelt's personal indecision about what policy his administration ought to follow in its relation with business."[5] Ironically, the commissioners concluded the New Deal had actually encouraged the growth of monopolies.

The decline of the New Deal had started with the economic downturn in 1937. It ended with the midterm elections of 1938. During those two years, the New Deal had shown both what it could and could not achieve in American politics. On a national level, FDR had endeared himself to voters as a champion of the people. Accordingly, he had easily won reelection in 1936. "But American laws

and customs do not provide for the national organization of politics," noted historian Eric Rauchway. "And against a Congress elected from localities, against a Senate elected from states, Roosevelt's cross-sectional politics foundered."[6]

In a sense, New Deal politics offered something for all. Powerful business forces—investment bankers, bankers, real-estate developers, building contractors, mass retailers, and more—benefited from its capitalism. Their weight balanced the growing influence of unions and party liberals. Likewise, southern Democrats, particularly those in Congress, blocked the party from moving too far to the left. Hard-line segregationists among them enacted legislation that weakened some New Deal reforms. (Key dilutions included exempting agricultural and domestic workers from protection under the Social Security Act and the National Labor Relations Act.) FDR fought back by endorsing their liberal opponents in the 1938 Democratic primaries. His strategy failed.

"As a result, the Democratic party emerged from this era divided between hopeful black masses, labor unionists, and liberals on the one hand and die-hard southern segregationists on the other," wrote historian Joseph A. McCartin. "Nonetheless, the political shifts of the New Deal Era awakened the hopes of previously subordinated groups in American society. Workers, radicals, blacks, and women alike enjoyed rising expectations."[7]

The New Deal's record on civil rights took the middle road. Many leading New Dealers, including Eleanor Roosevelt and Harry Hopkins, worked hard to ensure that African Americans received at least 10 percent of welfare assistance programs. (African Americans then made up 10 percent of the total U.S. population but 20 percent of the poor.) But relief programs ran segregated camps and often discriminated against African Americans. FDR appointed a record number of blacks to second-level posts in his administration. However, he refused to support anti-lynching legislation for fear of angering powerful southern Democrats. Under the New Dealers, African Americans took two steps forward and one back.

Similarly, women's causes advanced little under New Deal policies, but women gained significant influence in government. Feminist activist Molly Dewson worked hard to help Frances Perkins become the first woman to serve in a cabinet post (as secretary of labor). Perhaps no one did more for women than Eleanor Roosevelt. In promoting women's rights in her travels, writings, speeches, and participation in debates within the administration, she transformed the role of First Lady.

New Dealers brought some improvements to the Native American population. FDR appointed reformer John Collier to head the Bureau of Indian Affairs. He pushed a series of laws through Congress to aid Native American communities. The last of these, the Indian Reorganization Act of 1934, granted Native Americans the rights of self-government and cultural freedom on reservations.

Contrary to the misinformed belief of many Americans, the New Deal did not end the Great Depression. Soon after the New Deal had slipped away into history, World War II erupted in Europe on September 1, 1939. FDR had seen the signals and had already begun preparing for it. The phenomenal American industrial machine slipped into gear, cranking out the weapons and materials of war. Millions of unemployed Americans went back to work. By 1943, the Depression gave way to the most destructive war in the history of humankind.

Government posters used to motivate workers during the Great Depression proved equally effective in promoting World War II productivity.

The triumphs and failures of the New Deal remain subjective and depend largely on the political perspective of the beholder. Some may wonder just how new the New Deal left the American way of life. "When the New Deal was over, capitalism remained intact," wrote historian Howard Zinn. "The rich still controlled the nation's wealth, as well as its laws, courts, police, newspapers, churches, colleges. Enough help had been given to enough people to make Roosevelt a hero to millions, but the same system that had brought depression and crisis—the system of waste, of inequality, of concern for profit over human need—remained."[8]

Early in the twenty-first century, Americans again witnessed a collapsed stock market and a shattered economy. Washington offered the same big-spending solutions to the same economic problems, somehow expecting different results. The success or failure of massive government intervention awaits the judgment of time.

Financial crises of one kind or another—panics, recessions, and depressions—are nothing new in the world. Beginning in 1797, the United States alone has experienced at least twenty periods of prolonged economic instability. These episodes of declining prosperity have lasted as few as six months (in 2001) and as long as twenty-three years (from 1873 to 1896). Like the seasons, economic downturns seem cyclical in nature.

Arguably, the most severe of all U.S. depressions was the Great Depression of the 1930s. In that troubled decade, Americans witnessed some of the hardest times in their history. But they persevered and met the economic challenges of their time. In the end, the strength and resiliency of America's economy prevailed, and it prospered again. By 2008, Americans were facing a financial crisis of equal or even greater proportions.

Obama's approach to the modern financial crisis has a remarkable similarity to the New Deal.

That summer, oil prices reached an all-time high of $147.27 per barrel. Americans began to feel the monetary pinch at the gas pump. Summer moved on toward fall. In September, sub-prime mortgage lenders Fannie Mae and Freddie Mac began to implode. (Sub-prime mortgages are those granted to borrowers with high default rates and are thus considered risky investments.) The housing-market collapse caused available credit to dry up. Credit scarcity resulted in a liquidity crisis. Banks failed. Stock markets crashed worldwide. And finally the U.S. banking system failed.

Under President George W. Bush and Secretary of the Treasury Henry Paulson, Congress passed the $700 billion Troubled Assets Relief Program (TARP). This money was meant to buy up the bad assets (mostly mortgages) of financial institutions. In theory, once free of their bad assets, lenders would put "good" money back in circulation. Renewed liquidity would hopefully lead to available credit and economic recovery. The success or failure of TARP remains in question.

In February 2009, newly inaugurated President Barack Obama shepherded the $787 billion American Recovery and Investment Act through Congress. Obama's so-called stimulus plan was aimed at spending across a broad spectrum, including investing in new technologies that would provide jobs, and therefore improve the country's cash flow. The new president's philosophy relied largely on the power of money to spend America's way out of decline. Whatever the future holds, few gamblers would bet against the ability of Americans to bounce back.

Chronology

1882	Franklin Delano Roosevelt (FDR) is born to James and Sara Delano Roosevelt on January 30 in Hyde Park, New York.
1900–07	FDR attends Harvard University and Columbia Law School; he passes the New York bar examinations.
1905	FDR marries Eleanor Roosevelt on March 17.
1910–13	FDR serves in the New York State Senate.
1913–20	FDR serves as assistant secretary of the navy.
1921	Polio strikes FDR, crippling him for life.
1928	FDR is elected governor of New York.
1929	The stock market collapses on October 29, "Black Tuesday." The Great Depression begins.
1930	Congress enacts the Smoot-Hawley Tariff Act.
1932	Congress passes the Revenue Act and the Federal Home Loan Bank Act. President Herbert Hoover orders the dispersal of the Bonus Army in Washington, D.C. FDR accepts the Democratic nomination for president in July and defeats Hoover in the fall election.
1933	
March 4	FDR delivers his inaugural address in Washington, D.C. His first hundred days in office begins.
March 9	Congress passes Emergency Banking Act.
March 12	FDR airs his first fireside chat.
March 20	Congress passes the Economy Act.
March 22	Congress enacts the Beer-Wine Revenue Act.
March 31	Civilian Conservation Corps Reforestation Act is passed by Congress.
May 12	Congress establishes the Federal Emergency Relief Agency (FERA) and the Agricultural Adjustment Act.
May 18	Washington lawmakers create the Tennessee Valley Authority.
May 27	Securities Act passes Congress.
June 13	Lawmakers enact the Home Owners' Loan Act.
June 16	The Farm Credit Act, Banking Act (Glass-Steagall Act), and National Industrial Recovery Act (which creates the National Recovery Administration and the Public Works Administraion) are passed by Congress. FDR's first hundred days in office end.
November 9	FDR establishes the Civil Works Administration under Harry Hopkins.

Chronology

1934

June 6	Congress passes the Securities Exchange Act.
June 19	Lawmakers enact the Communications Act.
June 28	Congress approves the National Housing Act.

1935

April 8	Congress passes the Emergency Relief Appropriation Act, which authorizes the Works Progress Administration.
May 11	Legislators approve the Rural Electrification Act.
May 27	The Supreme Court strikes down the president's authority to remove members of the Federal Trade Commission and declares the National Recovery Administration unconstitutional.
July 5	Congress enacts the National Labor Relations Act (or Wagner Act).
August 14	Lawmakers pass the Social Security Act.
August 26	Congress enacts the Public Utility Holding Company Act.
August 30	The Revenue Act (better known as the "Wealth Tax") passes Congress.
September 9	Senator Huey Long of Louisiana is assassinated by political rival.

1936 FDR is elected to a second term as president.

1938

February 16	Congress passes the Agricultural Adjustment Act of 1938.
June 25	FDR wins passage of the Fair Labor Standards Act.
November	New Deal phases out with the midterm elections.

1939 War erupts in Europe on September 1.

1940 FDR is elected to a third term as president.

1941 Japanese bomb U.S. military installations at Pearl Harbor; United States enters World War II the next day.

1943 The Great Depression ends.

1944 FDR is elected to his fourth term as president.

1945 FDR dies of cerebral hemorrhage on April 12.

Timeline in History

1904	Construction begins on Panama Canal; it opens in 1914.
1909	Commander Robert E. Peary and Matthew Henson reach the North Pole.
1912	The *Titanic* collides with an iceberg and sinks in the North Atlantic.
1914	Archduke Franz Ferdinand, heir to the Austrian throne, and his wife are assassinated in Sarajevo; World War I begins.
1920	The Nineteenth Amendment gives U.S. women the right to vote.
1933	Adolf Hitler is appointed chancellor of Germany.
1936	Chiang Kai-shek declares war on Japan.
1939	Germany invades Poland; Britain and France declare war on Germany.
1941	The Japanese bomb U.S. naval base at Pearl Harbor on December 7; the United States joins the Allies in World War II the next day.
1945	Germany surrenders to the Allies on May 8; Japan capitulates on September 2; World War II ends.
1947	Congress passes the Twenty-second Amendment, which limits the U.S. president to two terms.
1948	The state of Israel is formed.
1950	North Korea invades South Korea, igniting the Korean War; fighting ends in 1953.
1954	RCA introduces the first color television.
1963	U.S. President John F. Kennedy is assassinated in Dallas, Texas.
1965	U.S. ground troops land in Vietnam.
1968	Martin Luther King Jr. is assassinated in Memphis, Tennessee.
1973	U.S. troops leave Vietnam.
1974	Watergate scandal forces U.S. President Richard M. Nixon to resign.
1977	United States agrees to return the Panama Canal to Panama.
1980	Japan surpasses the United States as the world's largest automobile manufacturer.
1981	IBM introduces the first personal computer.
1989	Thousands of students protest for democracy in Tiananmen Square, Beijing, China.
2001	Islamic terrorists attack the World Trade Center in New York City in two hijacked American aircraft and strike the Pentagon in Washington, D.C., in a third aircraft. A fourth hijacked airplane crashes in a Pennsylvania field.
2003	The U.S. invades Iraq based on intelligence that Saddam Hussein is concealing weapons of mass destruction (WMDs). The intelligence later proves faulty, and the WMDs are never found. Costs associated with the Second Iraq War contributes to U.S. deficit spending and later to the decline of the American economy.
2005	Iraqi people hold their first free election in more than fifty years.
2008	Congress authorizes $700 billion in bank aid as part of the Troubled Assets Recovery Plan in October. Barack H. Obama is elected as the forty-fourth president of the United States in November.
2009	Congress passes the $787 billion American Recovery and Reinvestment Act (better known as President Obama's stimulus plan).

Chapter Notes

Chapter 1. Good Times to Bad Times

1. Elliott V. Bell, "The Wall Street Crash, New York, 24 October 1929," in *The Mammoth Book of Eye-witness History*, edited by Jon E. Lewis (New York: Carroll & Graf Publishers, 1998), p. 368.
2. Ibid., p. 369.
3. Frederick Lewis Allen, *"CRASH!" in The Crash of 1929 and the Depression*, http://www.sagehistory.net/twenties/Crash.htm
4. Ibid.
5. Douglas G. Brinkley, *American Heritage History of the United States* (New York: Viking, 1998), p. 400.
6. Ibid., p. 401.
7. Michael E. Parrish, *Anxious Decades: America in Prosperity and Depression, 1920–1941* (New York: W. W. Norton, 1992), p. 257.

Chapter 2. FDR

1. Michael E. Parrish, *Anxious Decades: America in Prosperity and Depression, 1920–1941* (New York: W. W. Norton, 1992), pp. 270, 271.
2. William E. Leuchtenburg, *Franklin D. Roosevelt and the New Deal: 1932–1940* (New York: Harper & Row, 1963), p. 8.
3. Arthur M. Schlesinger Jr., *The Crisis of the Old Order: The Age of Roosevelt, 1919–1933* (New York: History Book Club, 2002), p. 322.
4. Ibid., p. 326.
5. Ibid., p. 328.
6. Ibid., p. 344.
7. Ibid., p. 385.
8. David M. Kennedy, *Freedom from Fear: The American People in Depression and War, 1929–1945* (New York: Oxford University Press, 1999), p. 134.
9. Schlesinger, p. 327.
10. Parrish, p. 275.

Chapter 3. The New Deal: The First Hundred Days

1. David M. Kennedy, *Freedom from Fear: The American People in Depression and War, 1929–1945* (New York: Oxford University Press, 1999), p. 134.
2. Douglas G. Brinkley, *American Heritage History of the United States* (New York: Viking, 1998), p. 409.
3. Michael E. Parrish, *Anxious Decades: America in Prosperity and Depression, 1920–1941* (New York: W. W. Norton, 1992), p. 292.
4. Brinkley, p. 409.
5. Arthur M. Schlesinger Jr., *The Coming of the New Deal, 1933–1935* (The Age of Roosevelt, vol. II) (Boston: Houghton Mifflin, 1986), p. 337.

6. Ibid., p. 166.
7. Parrish, p. 297.
8. Paul M. Johnson, *Modern Times: The World from the Twenties to the Nineties, rev. ed.* (New York: HarperCollins, 1991), p. 240.

Chapter 4. The New Deal: The Second Time Around

1. William E. Leuchtenburg, *Franklin D. Roosevelt and the New Deal: 1932–1940* (New York: Harper & Row, 1963), pp. 123–24.
2. Ibid., p. 124.
3. PBS, "People & Events: Franklin Delano Roosevelt,"http://www.pbs.org/wgbh/amex/dustbowl/peopleevents/pandeAMEX01.html
4. Ibid.
5. Arthur M. Schlesinger Jr., *The Coming of the New Deal, 1933–1935* (The Age of Roosevelt, vol. II) (Boston: Houghton Mifflin, 1986), p. 315.
6. Michael E. Parrish, *Anxious Decades: America in Prosperity and Depression, 1920–1941* (New York: W. W. Norton, 1992), p. 359.
7. David M. Kennedy, *Freedom from Fear: The American People in Depression and War, 1929–1945* (New York: Oxford University Press, 1999), p. 380.
8. Ibid., p. 222.
9. Leuchtenburg, p. 101.
10. Parrish, p. 323.

Chapter 5. The New American Way

1. David M. Kennedy, *Freedom from Fear: The American People in Depression and War, 1929–1945* (New York: Oxford University Press, 1999), p. 286.
2. Eric Rauchway, *The Great Depression & the New Deal: A Very Short Introduction* (New York: Oxford University Press, 2008), p. 115.
3. Ibid., p. 116.
4. Michael E. Parrish, *Anxious Decades: America in Prosperity and Depression, 1920–1941* (New York: W. W. Norton, 1992), p. 378.
5. William E. Leuchtenburg, *Franklin D. Roosevelt and the New Deal: 1932–1940* (New York: Harper & Row, 1963), p. 258.
6. Rauchway, p. 117.
7. Joseph A. McCartin, *"The New Deal Era,"* in *The Oxford Companion to United States History*, edited by Paul S. Boyer (New York: Oxford University Press, 2001), p. 548.
8. Howard Zinn, *A People's History of the United States: 1492–Present, Twentieth Anniversary ed.* (New York: HarperCollins, 1999), pp. 403–04.

Further Reading

For Young Readers

Allport, Alan. *Franklin Delano Roosevelt*. New York: Chelsea House, 2003.

Feinstein, Stephen. *The 1930s from the Great Depression to The Wizard of Oz*. Rev. ed. Berkeley Heights, NJ: Enslow Publishers, 2006.

Ford, Carin T. *Franklin D. Roosevelt: The 32nd President*. Berkeley Heights, NJ: Enslow Publishers, 2006.

Haugen, Brenda. *Franklin Delano Roosevelt: The New Deal President*. Mankato, MN: Capstone Press, 2006.

Nardo, Don. *The Great Depression*. Farmington Hills, MI: Lucent Books, 2007.

Uschan, Michael V. *The Importance of Franklin D. Roosevelt*. Farmington Hills, MI: Lucent Books, 2002.

Works Consulted

Badger, Anthony J. *The New Deal: The Depression Years, 1933–40*. Chicago: Ivan R. Dee, 2002.

Boyer, Paul S., ed. *The Oxford Companion to United States History*. New York: Oxford University Press, 2001.

Brinkley, Douglas G. *American Heritage History of the United States*. New York: Viking, 1998.

Faragher, John Mack, ed. *The American Heritage Encyclopedia of American History*. New York: Henry Holt, 1998.

Howard, Michael, and Wm. Roger Louis, eds. *The Oxford History of the Twentieth Century*. New York: Oxford University Press, 1998.

Johnson, Paul M. *A History of the American People*. New York: HarperCollins, 1997.

———. *Modern Times: The World from the Twenties to the Nineties*. Rev. ed. New York: HarperCollins, 1991.

Kennedy, David M. *Freedom from Fear: The American People in Depression and War, 1929–1945*. New York: Oxford University Press, 1999.

Kennedy, Paul. *The Rise and Fall of the Great Powers: Economic Change and Military Conflict from 1500 to 2000*. New York: Vintage Books, 1987.

Leuchtenburg, William E. *Franklin D. Roosevelt and the New Deal: 1932–1940*. New York: Harper & Row, 1963.

Lewis, Jon E., ed. *The Mammoth Book of Eyewitness History*. New York: Carroll & Graf Publishers, 1998.

Parrish, Michael E. *Anxious Decades: America in Prosperity and Depression, 1920–1941*. New York: W. W. Norton, 1992.

Powell, Jim. *FDR's Folly: How Roosevelt and His New Deal Prolonged the Great Depression*. New York: Three Rivers Press, 2004.

Rauchway, Eric. *The Great Depression & the New Deal: A Very Short Introduction*. New York: Oxford University Press, 2008.

Schlesinger, Arthur M., Jr. *The Coming of the New Deal, 1933–1935*. (The Age of Roosevelt, vol. II.) Boston: Houghton Mifflin, 1986.

———. *The Crisis of the Old Order: The Age of Roosevelt, 1919–1933*. New York: History Book Club, 2002.

Zinn, Howard. *A People's History of the United States: 1492–Present*. Twentieth Anniversary ed. New York: HarperCollins, 1999.

On the Internet

Library of Congress: The Learning Page, "Great Depression and World War II, 1929–1945: President Franklin Delano Roosevelt and the New Deal, 1933–1945"
http://memory.loc.gov/learn/features/timeline/depwwii/newdeal/newdeal.html

PBS: American Experience: Surviving the Dust Bowl, "People & Events: Franklin Delano Roosevelt"
http://www.pbs.org/wgbh/amex/dustbowl/peopleevents/pandeAMEX01.html

Sage History: The Crash of 1929 and the Depression
http://www.sagehistory.net/twenties/Crash.htm

Sage History: FDR and the New Deal
http://www.sagehistory.net/deprnewdeal/NewDealSummary.htm

Glossary

blacklist
To name as someone to be avoided, especially for employment.

bubble (BUH-bul)
A condition in the stock market when prices paid by investors surpass any reasonable expectation of future earnings.

capitalism (KAA-pih-tul-ih-zem)
An economic system in which trade and industry are controlled by private owners.

chancellor (CHAN-seh-lor)
The chief minister of state in some European countries.

conservator (kon-SUR-vuh-tor)
An official charged with the protection of something affecting public welfare and interests.

commodities (kuh-MAH-dih-tees)
Goods and services.

foreclosure (for-KLOH-jhur)
To end the terms of a mortgage agreement, with the property returning to the lender.

GNP
Gross National Product; the total market value of the goods and services produced by a nation's economy during a specific period of time, such as annually.

Good Neighbor Policy
U.S. policy fostering trade agreements between the Americas and renouncing U.S. right to intervene (especially militarily) in Latin American affairs.

liquidation (lih-kwih-DAY-shun)
The conversion of assets, such as stocks, into cash.

liquidity (lih-KWIH-dih-tee)
Able to cover current liabilities (expenses and debt) with current assets.

mandate (MAN-dayt)
An authorization to act given to a representative of the people.

monopoly (muh-NAH-puh-lee)
A market in which a seller has no competition.

New Deal
The legislative and administrative program of President Franklin D. Roosevelt designed to promote economic recovery and social reform in the 1930s.

noblesse oblige (noh-BLESS oh-BLEEZH)
The idea that privilege entails responsibility.

Prohibition (proh-ih-BIH-shun)
In the United States, the period from 1920 to 1933 in which it was illegal to manufacture, sell, or transport alcoholic beverages; initiated by the Eighteenth Amendment and repealed by the Twenty-first Amendment.

solvency
The state of being able to pay all legal debts.

tariff (TAYR-ef)
A duty (fee) required to be paid on imports or exports.

Index